THE
GOSPEL
OF
PAUL

THE GOSPEL OF PAUL

Robert B. Campbell

JUDSON PRESS, Valley Forge

THE GOSPEL OF PAUL

The contents of this book are based upon material first published in *Adult Class*, Volume 68, Number 1, published by the American Baptist Churches in the U.S.A., Board of Educational Ministries, Valley Forge, Pa.

Library of Congress Cataloging in Publication Data

Campbell, Robert C
    The Gospel of Paul.

    1. Bible. N. T. 1 Corinthians—Theology.
2. Bible. N. T. Romans—Theology. I. Title.
BS2675.2.635   227'.2   73-7582
ISBN 0-8170-0587-0

Printed in the U.S.A.

Preface

There is no want of excellent biblical scholarship in our day. The breadth and depth of research in biblical studies and related fields are greater than at any other time in human history.

Moreover, the best material available demands the kind of theological expertise and technical background which most people do not enjoy. The literature generally produced by scholars is aimed at other scholars. But most of us are ill prepared in background and interest to use the critical tools available for biblical study.

The great need is a bridge. In a measure this is provided by our pastors through biblical preaching. But there is all too little of even this. The layman who hungers for the Word of God and who looks for help in understanding Scripture must also be recognized.

This volume is an attempt at popularizing biblical scholarship. Its purpose is communicative. Short sentences are the order of the day. The obvious meaning of the biblical text is hopefully expounded with clarity.

The work is purposefully brief. It is hoped that these words will only be suggestive. If they guide the reader to a wrestling with the Bible itself, the efforts in writing will have been amply rewarded.

The sections here presented are highly selective. The biblical materials are limited to the selections from the two longest letters of Paul—Romans and First Corinthians. The gospel as understood by the apostle is clearly reflected in these two ancient letters.

These words relate to life. This was true in the day of their writing. If we are truly biblical, we shall similarly be life-oriented. These teachings relate to our experience and environment. They point to life. A new kind of life is desperately needed and deeply desired in our day. Admit it or not, we have a deep hunger for God. The Bible helps satisfy this need. It is a communication from life to life.

Robert C. Campbell

Contents

The Fractured Church

In this book we shall be dealing with the general theme of "The Gospel According to Paul." Our study will relate primarily to his letter to the Romans and to 1 Corinthians. In our present listing of the order of Paul's letters in the New Testament, these letters have the first and second place. This is because our present arrangement is according to the length of the letters. It is not surprising that the most of "The Gospel According to Paul" can be found in these most extensive and thorough of his writings.

This chapter relates to both of Paul's letters to Corinth. These letters reflect the divisions within the church at Corinth and the difficulties which existed between Paul and the church.

Problems in Corinth

The problems in the Corinthian church were many. On the one hand, we may be surprised to find that a church so near the time of our Lord and actually founded by the great apostle should be laden with problems. On the other hand, Corinth was an extremely wicked city. Hence we need not be surprised.

We recognize problems within our churches today. This often causes us to look back with longing eyes to the "good old days." We want to feel that we are a "New Testament church," without problems. Not so! The church at Corinth is clearly a church of the New Testament, but it could hardly be matched as a place of problems.

Consider their situation. Corinth was located on an isthmus which connects northern and southern Greece, just as Panama connects the North and South American continents on a grander scale. It was a "sailor's town." Many tourists were "out for a fling." Almost all the trade routes between Asia and Europe funneled through the city of Corinth. And through this funnel came the evils of both continents. Corinth was so evil that our modern English word "to corinthianize" means "to live sinfully."

Even the religion of Corinth was corrupt. In old Corinth the people could look up to the top of an adjacent mountain where there stood a temple to the goddess Aphrodite. This temple housed a thousand sacred priestesses who moved down to the city each night to serve as religious prostitutes. Even so, Paul had established a congregation of Christian people to whom he could write:

To the church of God which is at Corinth, to those sanctified in Christ Jesus, called to be saints . . . (1 Corinthians 1:2).

But "saints" are not perfect. All of us who know Jesus Christ as Lord and Savior are saints, but we have a long way to go before we are really like our Lord. This was certainly true of the Corinthians. Problems were rampant in the congregation. Paul reflects on disunity, incest, immorality, and lawsuits within the congregation. He deals with their confusion about the relations of the sexes, meat which may or may not be eaten, the problem of speaking in tongues and other spiritual gifts, and even their inability to take an offering correctly. Imagine a church that has to have instructions in how to take an offering! Nor were their problems all functional. There were some significant failures to understand basic Christian doctrine. Some of the people didn't even believe in Easter! Hence Paul could honestly ask,

How can some of you say that there is no resurrection of the dead? (1 Corinthians 15:12).

Divisions in Corinth

The primary problem of the church at Corinth was divisions within the fellowship. This is the great concern to which Paul writes in the first four chapters, and he may even be relating primarily to this problem in chapters 5 and 6.

I appeal . . . that there be no dissensions among you, but that you be united in the same mind and the same judgment (1 Corinthians 1:10).

Paul's appeal is that the cliques be stopped! He speaks

of them as "dissensions." This word in the original Greek is *schisma,* which is transliterated in our word *schism.* The word means a tear or a rip in an article of clothing. It makes the clothing both unattractive and without value unless it is properly mended. So with the church.

Paul's answer to these unsightly divisions within the Christian fellowship is that we be *united.* The word he uses is commonly used in Greek literature to describe the reweaving of a torn cloth or the mending of torn nets.

Our becoming united is to result in the "same *mind* and the same *judgment."* Our "mind" refers to our views or understandings. We should study Scripture with the purpose of attaining a unity of Christian view as reflected in our biblical faith. Our same *judgment* refers to the statements which we make as Christians. It is appropriate that we make our confessions of faith. It is also appropriate that we take a stand on the key social issues of our day. Such statements of belief or activity should reflect a unity of Christian mind. Where we disagree, however, we should do so pleasantly and not be involved in the divisions and quarrels which were reflected in the Corinthian congregation.

For . . . there is quarreling among you, my brethren (1 Corinthians 1:11).

Note that Paul refers to the Corinthians as "brethren" at the beginning of verse 10 and the conclusion of verse 11. He thereby encourages us to recognize our brother and relate to him in a loving manner, even if we disagree. But these people were unable to do that: "there is quarreling among you, my brethren." The word "quarreling" is the Greek word *Eris.* This is the name of the Greek goddess of strife. Hence Paul is referring to these people as actually having strife in their midst rather than reflecting the unity which is in our Lord Jesus Christ.

What I mean is that each one of you says, "I belong to Paul," or "I belong to Apollos," or "I belong to Cephas," or "I belong to Christ" (1 Corinthians 1:12).

There seem to be four divisions in the Corinthian church. The first group is related to Paul, emphasizing the freedom which Paul found so central to the gospel. The second group is related to Apollos, probably emphasizing a more "intellectual approach" to the Christian faith. A third group is related to Cephas (Peter), probably emphasizing the Jewish element of the Christian faith. Finally, there were those spiritually superior people who "put down" other groups and claimed that they alone followed the Lord.

Solutions for Divisions

Paul tactfully presented solutions, illustrating with the party which followed his particular name.

Is Christ divided? Was Paul crucified for you? Or were you baptized in the name of Paul? (1 Corinthians 1:13).

The first solution to division is to recognize that Christ is our only Savior.

A second solution is also to be found in Christ. He alone is the Head of the church. We were baptized only in his name—not in that of any other.

The problem of divisions among Christians is still with us. Moreover, these solutions are still valid. We are one with all who know Jesus Christ as Savior. We find our unity in him who is our Head.

When we Christians relate to each other from our different national and denominational backgrounds, we call this relationship the "ecumenical movement." (The Greek word *ecumene* means "the inhabited earth," so the term refers to all Christians everywhere.) We sense a unity even in our differences, because we are made one by Christ himself, our only Savior and Head.

But the problem remains. When Paul later wrote 2 Corinthians 12:19-21, he feared that there might still be "quarreling, jealousy, anger, selfishness," etc. This problem of division among Christians is a deep one. It was not easily solved in Paul's day—nor in ours!

God's Wisdom for Man's Folly

Over five hundred years ago a devoted Christian leader named Thomas à Kempis wrote in his book *The Imitation of Christ* a very practical bit of advice. He said, "To have a low opinion of our own merits and to think highly of others is an evidence of wisdom."

This appeal to sobriety was needed by the church at Corinth. They were divided because of their self-centered concerns. They needed the humbling wisdom of God which would unite their fellowship.

Two Kinds of Wisdom

Paul contrasts wisdom and folly in 1 Corinthians 1:18 and 2:8-9. Then he indicates how we can attain the wisdom of God through the Holy Spirit in 1 Corinthians 2:9-16.

The Folly and Power of the Cross

For the word of the cross is folly to those who are perishing, but to us who are being saved it is the power of God (1 Corinthians 1:18).

The heart of the gospel is the cross. It is an instrument of capital punishment comparable to the modern electric chair or gas chamber. Yet God has used this ugly thing to bring about our salvation. Yet, we think of the cross as a decorative piece. We beautify our churches and even our persons with crosses.

The Corinthians, however, did not view the cross in this sentimental way. Their sophisticated Greek neighbors were saying that it was ridiculous to believe that a crucified criminal could meet their souls' deep needs. Moreover, their Jewish friends could not conceive of God's Messiah as dying on a cross but rather as a ruler coming in power. To many Gentiles and Jews, Jesus' death was just so much foolishness.

But in answer to critics Paul was extremely pragmatic.

15

The cross worked! It really did save. He had experienced it. So had the Corinthians. And so have we.

The Wisdom of the World

Where is the wise man? Where is the scribe? Where is the debater of this age? Has not God made foolish the wisdom of the world? (1 Corinthians 1:20).

Paul reflects upon the wisdom of this world with a series of rhetorical questions which grow out of his quotation of Isaiah 29:14 in the previous verse. When Paul rhetorically asks *where* these various wise people are, the obvious answer is *nowhere*. Even the wisest of this world are nothing before God. The first question refers to the "wise man," the Sophist. Even today we speak of the world-wise person as "sophisticated." The second question relates to the wise leader in the Jewish community, the scribe. Even the wisdom which comes from Scripture as studied by the scribe needs to be understood in the light of the cross. The third question relates to the person who handles words with skill and wisdom, the debater. The intellectual leader of ancient or modern society may be a person whose antenna is not directed toward the things of God. Nothing of God comes through to him. He simply has no connection. Thus it is not strange that the things of God, and notably the cross, are so much foolishness when viewed in the light of the wisdom of this world.

The Wisdom of God

For since, in the wisdom of God, the world did not know God through wisdom, it pleased God through the folly of what we preach to save those who believe (1 Corinthians 1:21).

The ancients who claimed special wisdom (Sophists) or unique knowledge (Gnostics) had no inside track with God. Nor do we with our modern scientific knowledge. Our observation of God's world enables us to know something *about* him, but a personal knowledge of God is not a human attainment. If it were so, only the intellectuals could be related to God.

But God is too wise for that. He determined to meet us all in our deep need. Thus the true knowledge of God comes through the cross, not through creation. If we could know God intimately and fully through studying his creation, our relationship to him would depend upon our ability to understand all that goes on around us. But this relationship to God is based upon the cross. This can only reflect our response to God's great gift of his own Son.

> For Jews demand signs and Greeks seek wisdom, but we preach Christ crucified, a stumbling block to Jews and folly to Gentiles, but to those who are called, both Jews and Greeks, Christ the power of God and the wisdom of God (1 Corinthians 1:22-24).

Both the Jews and the Greeks of the first century demanded that Christ fit their pattern. The Greeks wanted to know God through their "wisdom," that is, through their philosophic speculation. On the other hand, the Jews demanded "signs," inasmuch as they wanted God's Messiah to prove clearly that he was the fulfillment of their expectations.

But Jesus disappointed both the Greeks and the Jews of this world. He was unacceptable to the Greeks because he refused to be a philosophic teacher fashioned to their liking. On the contrary, the gospel was "foolishness." Nor did he satisfy the Jews. Even on the cross he was challenged to come down so that they might believe. This would be a great "sign," but he gave them an even greater one. He came back from the dead after suffering the agony of the cross. Even then, they would not believe.

But the Christian (be he Jew or Greek) finds that Christ meets his deep needs. When we resign from our own achievements before God and our demands of God, we commit ourselves to him in simple faith. Then we find that Christ is "the power of God" which meets the Jewish need for "signs." And he is "the wisdom of God" truly needed by Greeks.

God's Wisdom Through God's Spirit

Not only are we to accept God's wisdom rather than man's, we are to accept God's way to wisdom rather than our own. God's way is not through our own understanding but through his revelation.

But as it is written,
"What no eye has seen, nor ear heard,
nor the heart of man conceived,
what God has prepared for those who love him"
(1 Corinthians 2:9).

This is not a funeral text, describing the life in the heavenly world. Paul is talking about the here and now. Indeed, he goes on:

God has revealed to us through the Spirit. For the Spirit searches everything, even the depths of God (1 Corinthians 2:10).

True spiritual knowledge does not come through the senses (eye and ear). It does not come through reason (man's conceiving). Rather it is "revealed to us through the Spirit." This is God's wisdom, not ours.

We have not attained to God. He rather came to us in his Son. Nor have we fully understood God. Rather he has revealed himself through the Spirit. More yet. God's Spirit has already begun teaching us the ultimate and deep things of God. We are in the Spirit and he is in us, so we begin to sense this deeper knowledge even now.

For what person knows a man's thoughts except the spirit of the man which is in him? So also no one comprehends the thoughts of God except the Spirit of God (1 Corinthians 2:11).

The only way any of us can know another person is to have that person reveal himself to us. You may know something *about* the people you observe and with whom you relate. But true insights as to their feelings, desires, hurts, ultimate concerns—these come only as a person opens himself to you.

So it is with God. God makes himself more clearly known to us through his Spirit. But we should note that the relation of the Holy Spirit to God is not identical with the relation which your spirit has to you. The Spirit is as personal as is the Father and the Son, and he teaches us at a personal level.

Unity at the Lord's Table

Strange thing; we are often most divided over that which best unites us. Witness tense marriages. Consider the fellowship of the church.

So the Lord's Supper—the communion service. The church of our Lord is really divided on this one. The Roman Catholic fellowship contends that the bread literally becomes the flesh of Christ, and the wine really is blood, including corpuscles. The Eastern Orthodox Church approximates this position. The Lutherans have modified the view. Many others have rejected it. So we have some of our deepest theological arguments about the meaning of communion.

It is more than our viewpoints which divide us. Many churches will not allow another Christian to observe communion with them. It is true of Roman Catholics and Episcopalians on the one hand, and it is also true of some Baptists. Christians are never so divided as at the communion table.

The communion also unites us. We recognize the first Sunday of October as World Wide Communion Sunday. Every Christian church which observes communion at any time sets this particular Sunday aside for this observation. With all our divisions, we find ourselves one in this great act of remembering our Lord and his suffering.

Contention Is Condemned (1 Corinthians 11:17-19)

Our lack of unity as Christians is not something new. Some of us plaintively wish for the "good old days" of the perfect unity of the New Testament church. Don't you believe it! The church at Corinth was a manifestation of the New Testament church. And was it ever divided! They followed different human leaders—some Paul, some Apollos, some Peter, and so forth (1 Corinthians 1:12-16; 3:4-9; 4:6). They maintained their class

19

distinctions. Individual Christians related only to the other Christians who happened to be in their particular social grouping.

> . . . I do not commend you, because when you come together . . . there are divisions among you (1 Corinthians 11:17-18).

The Corinthians could "come together," but they were not really together. They maintained rigid divisions in their life outside the church. There were racial divisions, economic divisions, social divisions, political divisions—Jew and Gentile, slave and free, Greek and barbarian, Roman citizen and noncitizen.

But in the church they were one. This was especially true at the communion table where they were reminded that distinctions of race and class were gone. They were all one at the foot of the cross as they remembered their Lord. They were a new kind of society in which people were really united and truly loved one another.

However, the Corinthians denied this unity and love. There were different cliques within the fellowship. They were one in Christ, but their actions and attitudes denied this unity. Paul could only condemn this denial. It was more than a lack of courtesy. It was a rejection of the unifying power of the cross.

Confusion Is Corrected (1 Corinthians 11:20-22, 27)

Blessed is the congregation that enjoys fellowship dinners. We call them "potluck" or (preferably) "share a dish" dinners. The Corinthians called it the Love Feast.

Each individual or family brought a particular dish or item of food, and all such items were shared in a common meal. The last part of the Love Feast was the sharing of the bread and cup in the Lord's Supper. It was a meaningful custom which reflected both their communion with Christ and their fellowship with one another.

But the corruption of the Corinthian church was focused in the communion service. Love was absent from the Love Feast. There was not true sharing in the "share a dish" dinners. Each family brought its own picnic dinner and ate with its own intimate friends.

This lack of love became climactic in the condition of a slave. Here was a man or woman who had found the one group in all the world where he felt genuinely human. He was really accepted as a person by his fellow Christians, because he had been accepted as God's child through Christ. But this acceptance was denied at the Love Feast. He had been about his chores all day, and he arrived late for the meal, hungry and weary. He stood waiting for an invitation to eat with others, but no such invitation was extended. The social rejection which he knew in all of life was also manifest there. The Corinthians spoke of unity, but they were not demonstrating it.

We are confused sometimes over that problem of inclusion of others, and at other times we are confused in a different direction—the inclusion of ourselves. We have separated the communion service from a common meal. We have made it special, and have related it exclusively to the hour of worship. We read that:

Whoever, therefore, eats the bread or drinks the cup of the Lord in an unworthy manner will be guilty . . . any one who eats and drinks without discerning the body eats and drinks judgment upon himself (1 Corinthians 11:27, 29),

and we wonder if we should approach the table. But Paul is not speaking about our *being worthy*. He is rather speaking of *eating in a worthy manner*. None of us is worthy. We are all sinners, and we are acceptable only in the light of the cross. It is precisely for this reason that we must not reject any other person. If we do so, we do not "discern the body." The body is both that of our Lord upon the cross *and* the church, his body today. Our denial of our brother is a splitting of the body and a rejection of our Lord.

Communion Is Commended (1 Corinthians 11:23-25)

Paul recalls the original circumstances of the Supper as given by our Lord. It is interesting to note that he actually wrote this letter to the Corinthians before any of our gospels were written. Hence this is actually our earliest written account of the institution of the Lord's Supper.

> When you meet together, it is not the Lord's supper that you eat.... I received from the Lord what I also delivered to you (1 Corinthians 11:20, 23).

The Corinthians had so changed the function involved in the communion service that they could no longer properly refer to their service as the Lord's Supper. It was rather their own supper, and it would have been better had they eaten it in their own homes.

But Paul was not satisfied simply to point up the error of their ways. Nor was he satisfied to compromise with them. He rather determined to strive for something higher. Indeed, he recalled for them precisely what he had received from the Lord. He pointed out the spirit and purpose of the original Lord's Supper with a view to helping them (and us) to enter into this kind of experience.

The original Lord's Supper as established by our Lord with his disciples was a Passover feast. The Passover meal as practiced even today by our Jewish friends begins with a question. The youngest male member present asks, "Why is this night different from all the other nights of the year?" The oldest man present then recites the acts of God by which he delivered his people from bondage. This probably happened at the first supper also, but Jesus went on to indicate that the great act of God's redemption was to take place the next day in the giving of his own body and blood for us. Now Paul recites the great work of Christ in our behalf by recalling the essential words of our Lord concerning his own body and blood.

In the Lord's Supper we relate to Christ in the past, present, and future. We recall his past sacrifice "in remembrance" (1 Corinthians 11:24), and in the present we "proclaim the Lord's death" (1 Corinthians 11:26) dramatically in the emblems of the bread and cup. Moreover, we relate to the future when "he comes" (1 Corinthians 11:26), and when our unity with him and our fellow Christians will be complete.

The Ministry of Reconciliation

All that God has done for us in Jesus Christ is beyond human explanation. The Bible gives us many models or pictures of Christ's work for us, but no single picture completely describes this great work. If we picture ourselves as lost, the Bible declares that Christ saved us. If we see ourselves as guilty, Christ has justified us. If we are unclean, we have been cleansed. If we are in bondage, we are redeemed. If we are defiled, we are sanctified. The pictures of our need and Christ's meeting of our need are almost numberless.

Probably the most meaningful model of Christ's work is the subject of this chapter—reconciliation. Our great need today is to be reconciled. We sense our estrangement, our emptiness, our meaningless life. We need to belong, to relate. We need reconciliation.

Reconciliation was needed in Paul's day. People were alienated from one another. There was alienation between the Jews and Gentiles, the Greeks and Romans, the Jews and Samaritans, the Pharisees and Sadducees, the free men and slaves—almost every conceivable group.

We also are estranged. We sense a lack of relationship with God. We know that we are apart from other people at any deep level. We even feel alienated from our true selves. Our great need is reconciliation.

Christ Brings Reconciliation (2 Corinthians 5:16-19)

Inasmuch as God has "reconciled us to himself," we are "in Christ" (2 Corinthians 5:18, 17). Paul refers to our being "in Christ" some one hundred seventy times in his letters. This is his favorite expression of what it means to be a Christian. This phrase which reflects our intimate relationship with the risen Lord cannot be superseded as an expression of reconciliation. We are no longer alone.

... though we once regarded Christ from a human point of view, we regard him thus no longer (2 Corinthians 5:16).

23

Paul once felt that Jesus was simply a Jewish renegade who had been shamefully crucified by the Romans. He now recognizes that he is the divine Lord who has become the head of a new community of faith and who has made all things new for his followers. Saul of Tarsus gave all his efforts to destroying the memory of Jesus, but Paul the apostle found in Christ the relationship with God for which he had always sought. He found this relationship beyond his grasp until it was freely given him in Jesus Christ.

Therefore, if any one is in Christ, he is a new creation; the old has passed away, behold, the new has come (2 Corinthians 5:17).

Things were radically changed for Paul, and they should be for us. The old attempts to please God with human merit were gone. So were the old human distinctions, the old motivations toward self-aggrandizement, the old human pride, the old hypocrisies; all was new.

But this new life is more than idealism and aspiration. It is daily experience. As we continue to live in Christ, things become increasingly renewed. The day will ultimately come, then, when we shall be in his presence and hear him say,

"Behold, I make all things new" (Revelation 21:5).

Ministers Preach Reconciliation (2 Corinthians 5:20-21)

We are not called to be reconciled to Christ. We are also called to be reconcilers for Christ. We have become believers, but we have also become ministers. Our Lord

. . . reconciled us to himself and gave us the ministry of reconciliation (2 Corinthians 5:18).

This ministry involves both a *mandate* and a *message*.

So we are ambassadors for Christ, God making his appeal through us (2 Corinthians 5:20).

Our mandate is to be ambassadors. In Paul's day an ambassador might represent either the Roman emperor or the Senate of Rome.

An ambassador of Caesar was the emperor's personal

representative who administered an area in the emperor's behalf. He was given the authority of the emperor, and Roman troops were at his disposal for upholding imperial power. He had a commission, and he spoke for Caesar himself. Paul conceived of himself and us as directly representing Christ as his ambassadors.

The Senate of Rome also had its ambassadors. When it was determined by the Senate that a conquered country should become a Roman province, the Senate dispatched ambassadors who arranged the terms for peace and for the continuing government of the newly created Roman province. They then returned to Rome in order to secure the Senate's ratification of these details. Thus these ambassadors were involved in bringing other people into a relationship with Rome. Again, Paul saw himself, and us, as Christ's ambassadors who proclaim Christ's peace in the gospel and who bring men into a vital relationship with the living God.

Honorable and responsible as is the position of ambassador, we are still servants. "We beseech" (2 Corinthians 5:20) men to be reconciled. We serve the world in the earnest hope that our efforts will lead them to know our Lord.

. . . be reconciled to God. For our sake he made him to be sin who knew no sin, so that in him we might become the righteousness of God (2 Corinthians 5:20-21).

Our *message* is one of reconciliation—that men "be reconciled to God." People are estranged. They cannot feel acceptable before God. Indeed, none of us is acceptable in his own right. Nevertheless, God has accepted us. He has given his Son for us. Our message to men is that they should accept their acceptance. Christ has already made their reconciliation possible. They must now accept and act upon this reconciliation. God has not turned his back upon them. He has come to them with a vital offer of relationship through his Son.

The Greek word for "reconciliation" also means "exchange." The message of reconciliation in Christ involves an exchange in Christ. He has become as we are, in order that we might become as he is. We are sinners, and

God has "made him to be sin." Note that Paul does not say that God has "made him a sinner." Our Lord is sinless, but he has accepted our sin so that we might be accepted with God. He has even made it possible "that in him we might become the righteousness of God." When we are reconciled to God, it is as his children who have been made like his only begotten Son.

We Need Reconciliation (2 Corinthians 6:1-2)

Christ has established our reconciliation with God. Such reconciliation is available only as it is known and received. Hence we have been called to spread the message of reconciliation. Even when this message is understood, it is effective only if it is acted upon. It is possible for us to understand the theological implications of Jesus' sacrifice and still not be reconciled. Reconciliation is a matter of will and personal commitment, not simply intellectual understanding.

. . . we entreat you not to accept the grace of God in vain (2 Corinthians 6:1).

Our acceptance of God's goodness in Christ makes his work effective in our behalf. We thereby enter the "grace of God" and find salvation. Every other person who enters this experience is our brother. Our reconciliation with God also reconciles us with our brother.

We not only need to accept our acceptance with God, we also desperately need to find reconciliation with our Christian brothers. If a person belongs to another denomination, if he has a different form of church government, if he does not understand the meaning or practice the form of baptism which I have, he is still my brother. The reconciliation which we have in Christ is not based upon our understanding or practice. It is based upon our faith. Every person who trusts Christ is our brother, and we must recognize our oneness with him. Thus we must be reconciled.

What Is the Gospel?

In this chapter we shall begin the study of Paul's letter to the Romans. The letter was written from Corinth on Paul's third missionary journey. It was written to a congregation which Paul had not seen, but these words were to serve as an introduction to the apostle's thinking as he anticipated a visit to Rome, which he hoped to make in the near future (Romans 15:23-24).

Romans is at once the fullest and most systematic presentation of the gospel to be found in the New Testament. We cannot do better than study this particular book if we are to understand what the gospel really is.

Good News!

The *gospel* is "good news." The Greek word for gospel originally used in the New Testament is transliterated into English as our word "evangel." The first two letters of this word mean "good." The word "angel" relates to "message" or "messenger" (an "angel" in Scripture is a messenger of God).

We use the word "gospel" more often than "evangel" today because of our dependence upon old English. Our word "gospel" comes from the older "God's spell," which meant "good story" or "God's story." Thus our word "gospel" means the good news of God's love for us shown in his only begotten Son.

> . . . I am not ashamed of the gospel . . . (Romans 1:16).

In the immediately preceding verses Paul has made it clear that he wants to preach the gospel in Rome.

> I long to see you. . . . I have often intended to come to you. . . . I am under obligation . . . so I am eager to preach the gospel to you also who are in Rome (verses 11, 13, 14, 15).

But a sophisticated Roman might object. "Not here, Paul! We are the intellectual and philosophical center of the world. Come up with something better than that story about the cross!" But Paul would have none of it.

> . . . it is the power of God for salvation to every one who has faith . . . (Romans 1:16).

The gospel was good news of the power of salvation, just as it is today. The message of Jesus and his cross is more than a story. It grabs us. Out of his death we find new life. Thus it is *good news!* Moreover, it is *power.* It works powerfully in changing our lives.

Seeing God's Righteousness

This salvation is both *from* something and *to* something. Paul indicates that we are saved *to* the righteousness of God.

> For in it the righteousness of God is revealed through faith (Romans 1:17).

These words constitute the theme of Paul's letter to the Romans. One cannot improve upon a six-word summary of this entire letter:

> . . . the righteousness of God . . . through faith (verse 17).

The three great emphases of this letter relate to these words. First, this righteousness of God is over against our sin and lack of righteousness (Romans 1:1—3:20). Second, this righteousness of God is given to us through faith and makes us acceptable to God for time and eternity (Romans 3:21—11:36). Third, this righteousness of God is effective in our life here and now (Romans 12:1—16:27).

We should see "righteousness" both as an *attribute* and an *activity* of God. Righteousness is both what God *is* and what he *does.*

On the one hand, God's righteousness simply means being "in the right," and Paul claims that God put us "in the right" also.

Our need for being "in the right" is clearly shown and given to us in our Lord's death for us. Thus this attribute of God of being "in the right" becomes our situation. We are now acceptable. This is good news!

On the other hand, the gospel reveals what God *does* for

us. God declares us "in the right" when we don't deserve it. This is obviously good news, but it may appear to make God seem less than righteousness. He should condemn us, should he not? But this is the good news. God has accepted our condemnation in his Son. He has stood by us in our great need, and he has supplied our need. His righteousness is shown in his not leaving us alone. It is also shown in his taking the hard way out of our sinful predicament—even the death of his own Son.

Seeing God's Wrath

We have noted that our salvation is *to* "the righteousness of God." This salvation is *from* "the wrath of God" (Romans 1:18).

The term "wrath of God" may bother us. Perhaps rightly so. We should remember that this is one of those few places in the New Testament where wrath is personally associated with God. Usually the mention of wrath is impersonally stated. It is called "the wrath to come," "the day of wrath," or simply "wrath."

But there is another side to this. Indeed, "the wrath of God" may be considered the opposite side of "the righteousness of God." This is a moral universe. The New Testament is clear about this. God is eternally hostile to the evil which would destroy us. The things which would ultimately take us away from God lead us to moral breakdown and our own destruction. And God is concerned. His concern reflects itself in wrath. The Lamb of God came to take away our sin, but the Bible ultimately refers to the strange picture of "the wrath of the Lamb" (Revelation 6:16).

For the wrath of God is revealed (Romans 1:18).

The wording is the same as the previous verse. In the gospel God's *righteousness* is revealed. In our sin which necessitates the gospel, the *wrath* of God is revealed. If God is truly righteous, he must react negatively against the evil which would destroy us. And he does. God gives us the freedom to choose evil, but even after our wrong choice he comes in love to make it possible for us to return to him as the prodigal son returned to his father.

For what can be known about God is plain . . . his eternal power and deity (Romans 1:19-20).

We can see God in nature. But we cannot know about God's love in nature. We can only know that there is an intelligent and powerful God over us as we observe nature. The only way we can know that God truly loves us is in the cross. Nature is "red of tooth and claw." But the cross demonstrates God's concern for us even in our sins. We can appreciate God in the forest, beside the babbling brook, or on a golf course. But we can only know God personally by responding to his love which was shown at Calvary.

. . . although they knew God they did not honor him as God (Romans 1:21).

The history of man is one of refusal to live up to the light which he has. God has let us know much about him in nature. Our history has been one of reacting with indifference. Then we move to speculate about God quite apart from his concrete revelation. Ultimately we are then blinded by our own ignorance and man's "senseless minds were darkened" (Romans 1:21).

Therefore God gave them up in the lusts of their hearts to impurity (Romans 1:24).

Paul describes our human history as a movement away from God. Our refusal to respond to God's revelation of himself in nature has led us to unbelief. Unbelief, in turn, has led us to immorality. When we did not conceive of God as central to our existence, we have refused to act as if God related to us at all. As we act without God, we have become more careless of one another. It is not strange, therefore, that the wrath stands over against us. The only answer is his righteousness revealed in the gospel.

But let us not forget. This only answer is also the *adequate* answer. Paul portrays our need of God in dark, bold, and foreboding strokes. But all this is in the light of God's great good news. We are his children in Christ— for time and eternity.

Law and Gospel

We really can't believe it. God accepts us when we are unacceptable. God makes us acceptable. This is good news—gospel. But it is natural for us to think the other way. We are legalists. We want to prove ourselves. We feel that we must earn our acceptance with God. But it can't be done. We can't meet the demands of the law. Only the gospel will do. Good news! This passage will help us to see the difference between the law (which we cannot achieve properly) and the gospel (which we must accept if we are to be acceptable).

Why We Are Unacceptable: The Law (Romans 3:19-20)

The term "the law" has several different meanings in the Bible. Two of these meanings are seen in the passage before us. In verse 19 Paul refers to the Old Testament as "the law," and he says that "it speaks" to us. "The law" originally referred to the first five books of the Old Testament, which the Jewish people referred to as *Torah* (the Hebrew word for "law"). The law of Moses (the Ten Commandments) is contained in these books, and this great section of Scripture is the full expression of the law of God reflected in the Ten Commandments.

The Jewish people thought of the Hebrew Bible (our Old Testament) as being made up of three sections: the Law, the Writings, and the Prophets. The Old Testament is often referred to in just two of these categories: "the Law and the Prophets." In this particular passage, however, Paul refers to the entire Old Testament (including the Prophets) as "the Law." He refers to the book of Isaiah and the Psalms as well as Moses in his extensive quotations of the previous verses (verses 10-18).

In verse 20, however, Paul refers to "the Law" as "works." Here the law is not Scripture. It is rather a legal way of being saved. For this reason Paul is both positive and negative about the law. He accepts Scripture. But he

31

refuses to accept the law as a way of salvation. The law is unable to save us, because we cannot keep the law. The law demands perfection. We simply cannot make it. Legalism, no! The gospel, yes! The law cannot save. It makes us see our need of salvation. It makes us aware of our sin, so we can respond to the gospel.

... the law ... speaks ... so that every mouth may be stopped, and the whole world may be held accountable to God (Romans 3:19).

A minister of the last generation commonly confronted people with the shocking question, "What would you do if you were to die immediately and stand before God and hear his question, 'What right do you have to come into my heaven?'" People who were so confronted were generally embarrassed and tried to dodge the question. When he pressed them, however, he received an answer something like, "Darned if I know what I would say to God." The minister then wisely referred such a person to this passage and pointed out that such an answer was in agreement with Paul. If one says, "Darned if I know," then his mouth has been stopped!

Paul then pronounced the sentence. The world is "accountable to God." We are guilty. The law points out why we are unacceptable, because

... through the law comes the knowledge of sin (verse 20).

How We Are Accepted: The Gospel (Romans 3:21-26)

God's righteousness is revealed to us both negatively and positively. Negatively speaking,

... the righteousness of God has been manifested apart from law (verse 21).

Positively speaking, what has been manifested is

the righteousness of God through faith in Jesus Christ for all who believe (verse 22).

The law demands righteousness. We *cannot* make it. Thus God's righteousness does not come by keeping the law. The gospel demands faith. We *can* respond to God's gift in trust. Thus the righteousness of God comes to us in the gospel.

Note that God's "righteousness" is in contrast with both our unrighteousness and our righteousness. God's righteousness is not only the opposite of our sins. It is also the opposite of our goodnesses. Even our goodnesses are not up to God's level of righteousness. Thus we plug into God's righteousness through faith.

Paul now positively describes how we are accepted in Christ. He uses three metaphors to explain what Christ has done for us. The first metaphor relates to a law court. The second relates to the ancient institution of slavery. The third relates to the sacrifices offered in the temple.

They are justified by his grace as a gift . . . (Romans 3:24).

The word "justify" means "to make clear, to acquit." The picture is that of a law court. To be justified is to hear the judge or foreman of the jury say, "Not guilty! In this metaphor of the law court God is seen as the judge. But he is a judge who acquits us "by his grace as a gift." This is strange! A judge is supposed to work on the basis of law, not of his gracious spirit. He is to dispense justice, not gifts. But that is the point. God is not simply a judge. He is rather one who declares us "not guilty" when we actually are guilty:

. . . through the redemption which is in Christ Jesus (Romans 3:24).

The word "redemption" does not mean too much to us today. We speak of savings-stamp stores as "redemption centers," and we may receive cash for "redemption" of a bond which has matured. Paul was referring to the ancient practice of slavery. We are now pictured as being on a slave auction block. We are in bondage to our sins, but Christ pays the price of our "redemption" and sets us free; he was the one

whom God put forward as an expiation by his blood . . . (Romans 3:25).

Paul now turns to the sacrifices offered in the temple as the picture through which we are to understand what Christ has done on the cross. "His blood" is his life which was given for us. He is seen as the sacrifice who has been given in our place to release us from the guilt of our sins.

The word here translated as "expiation" can also be translated "propitiation" or "mercy seat." Any of these three terms may do and each gives us a different picture of what Christ has done for us. As our "expiation" he has erased the guilt of our sin. As our "propitiation" he has appeased God's wrath toward our sins. As the "mercy seat" he is the place where God meets us with forgiveness of sin. ("The mercy seat" was the ark of the covenant in the "most holy place" of the Jewish temple. This is where God forgave all the sins of all the people each year on the Day of Atonement, or Yom Kippur.)

All of this is to say that Paul has used several pictures in order to show one great truth. This truth is that God has fully accepted us in spite of our sins. What Christ has done for us is gospel—good news!

Accepting Our Acceptance (Romans 3:27-28)

We feel that we are accepted only if we have proved ourselves. If we prove ourselves, we feel that we can boast of our achievement. But Paul rejects this. The Jews did not achieve acceptance by keeping the Ten Commandments. We do not achieve acceptance by being good neighbors, good citizens, or even good church members.

Then what becomes of our boasting? It is excluded. . . . (Romans 3:27)

We must simply accept the fact that God has accepted us in Christ. The Christian church is the one society into which a person enters by admitting that he is unworthy. We are not a fellowship of the elite. We do not claim to be the good people of the world. We are sinners who have been accepted in spite of ourselves. We are bad people who have been made good by God's love. We cannot boast of being special people. We can only witness to the special love which God has made clear to us in his Son.

Reconciliation Through Christ

This chapter focuses on how God reconciles us to himself through Christ. In chapter 4 we dealt with "the ministry of reconciliation." The primary thrust in that chapter was upon our communicating Christ's reconciliation to others. The emphasis here is upon how God has made this reconciliation possible.

Theologians refer to this emphasis as the Christian doctrine of the atonement. The word refers to "at-one-ment." Through Christ's death we are "atone" with God.

Through Rightness to Reconciliation

In the Scripture text of Romans 5:1-11, the first of these verses indicates that we have been "justified." The last verse indicates that "we have now received our reconciliation." To be "justified" means to be made "right with God." To be "reconciled" refers to a reestablishment of a previously broken relationship with God.

We are *justified* in relationship to *law*. We have broken God's law and have failed to do his will. Hence we are guilty. In being made "right with God," we are like a criminal who has been acquitted of a crime. Note that a judge never *makes* a person innocent. A judge rather *declares* one innocent. A person may be a guilty criminal but it is still possible to be acquitted of a crime. Thus the person is made "right with society." This is the legal status, and it may or may not reflect the actual fact of whether or not he committed the crime. So we. We are "right with God," justified, even though in actuality we have broken God's law.

God has established our rightness with him. This means that we are back in relationship with him. To be so related is *reconciliation*. This term is personal, whereas the term "justification" is legal. We are justified before God's law (legally), and we are reconciled to God himself (personally).

35

Present Results of Our Rightness

Therefore, since we are justified by faith, we have peace with God . . . we have obtained access . . . we rejoice in our hope . . . (Romans 5:1-2).

Paul describes our past, present, and future as Christians. Our past involves a justification already received. Our present reflects "peace with God." Our future is "hope of sharing the glory of God." Since we have already been "justified," we now live in peace with God and enjoy "access" to him. One day we shall actually share his glory.

When Paul indicates that "we have obtained access to this grace," he uses a word which means "a haven" or "a harbor" for a ship which is endangered by storm. On other occasions the word here translated "access" was used by the Greeks to refer to an "ushering" into the presence of a royal person. The picture is an audience in the presence of God himself.

Although Paul relates to our past justification and anticipates our future glory, his emphasis is upon the present in the first four verses of Romans 5. Here he speaks of our salvation as it is now. In verses 5-11 he emphasizes what our salvation will be then.

Rejoicing with Regard to the Future Despite Rejection

More than that, we rejoice in our sufferings. . . . (Romans 5:3).

In the immediately preceding words Paul has anticipated "our hope," and he indicates that we rejoice in this hope. But he anticipates an objection to this. One might rightly say, "Of course you rejoice in this hope of future glory. But that's all it is—a hope! It is a bubble which will burst when you arrive."

Paul answers the objection. We not only rejoice in that future hope. Even in the most difficult present circumstances "we rejoice in our sufferings." But why? How can we make sense of suffering? Well, perhaps we cannot, intellectually and rationally. But Scripture indicates how we can *respond* to suffering. We can act in a Christlike way even when we do not understand. Then some values come even from the evil of suffering. The difference is not in circumstances. The difference is within us. If we are committed to Christ and sense his strength in the midst of our suffering, then we find "suffering produces endurance." We learn to bear up with the strengthening of Christ within, and we can handle the load of suffering thrust upon us. Moreover, such "endurance produces character." The one who learns habitually to endure suffering in a Christlike way develops a Christlike character. Beyond this, Paul indicates that "character produces hope." Otherwise there is no sense in any suffering in the universe. If a strong character which can bear up under difficult circumstances is a good thing, then we must anticipate that there will be a future recognition of that good. This recognition by God in the future produces hope within us even in the present.

Now Paul has come around full circle. We are back to *hope*. Rejection and suffering we know. But within is hope. And it has substance. This "hope does not disappoint us" because God's love has already been shown to us. Our future hope is secure, because it is already rooted in our present experience and knowledge of the love of God. We may not know what the future holds, but we do know him who holds the future, and he is love.

Rejoicing in Recollection

Our present knowledge of God's love is rooted in the past demonstration of God's love on the cross. We were not worthy. On the contrary,

. . . we were yet helpless . . . we were yet sinners (Romans 5:6, 8).

Why, one will hardly die for a righteous man—though perhaps for a good man one will dare even to die. But God shows his love for us in that while we were yet sinners Christ died for us (Romans 5:7-8).

It's true. Would you die for a person who is perfect and self-contained? Hardly! On the other hand, someone just might be willing to die for a "good man" in the sense of loving children, caring for animals, and being helpful and supportive to those all about him.

But note the contrast. It is not when we were righteous or good. It was "while we were yet sinners" that our Lord died for us.

Rejoicing in Reassurance Regarding Future Judgment

We rejoice also in the future. God's love demonstrated in the past will be consummated in the future.

... now that we are reconciled, shall we be saved by his life (Romans 5:10).

If Christ gave his life for us when we were on the outside, we can be sure of his carrying us through future judgment now that we are on the inside. Our future is secure.

Not only so, but we also rejoice in God through our Lord Jesus Christ, through whom we have now received our reconciliation (Romans 5:11).

The Christian faith is more than a knowledge of the past and a hope about the future. It is even more than an understanding of our present experience. The Christian faith is ultimately a personal relationship. More than anything else, to be a Christian is to be related to God through his Son. Thus our ultimate rejoicing is not in the glorious hope of the future or God's giving meaning to our present difficulties. Our greatest rejoicing is in God himself. We really do know his presence. And it is our rejoicing as we look forward to that great day.

Free but Still Bound

We are saved by grace, and we live under grace. Grace is God's favor which freely forgives our sins.

This creates a problem. If God forgives us, then are we not free to live any way we wish? Isn't this kind of freedom dangerous?

These questions were asked in Paul's day. In Romans 6:1 the question is,

Are we to continue in sin that grace may abound?

The answer is a resounding *no*. This would contradict the meaning of our baptism. Thus Paul tells us in Romans 6:11 *how* we have been brought into a new life through Christ's death and *why* we should live this new kind of life. Then verses 12-14 tell us *how* to live this new kind of life each day. This leads to a second question:

Are we to sin because we are not under law but under grace? (Verse 15).

Again the answer is clearly *no*. Paul explains the answer to this question by changing the picture from that of baptism to the institution of slavery as practiced in his day.

Whose Slave Are You?

Paul commonly used human illustrations in order to communicate the truth of the gospel. He apologized for

. . . speaking in human terms, because of your natural limitations (Romans 6:19).

His apology might be extended for two further reasons. First, the illustration of slavery does not perfectly communicate our relationship to Christ. No illustration is perfect. Second, the illustration of slavery is embarrassing to us, inasmuch as we no longer recognize this evil practice. It is important to note that Paul is not condoning the practice. He is simply using a fact of first-century life to illustrate a great spiritual truth.

> Do you not know that if you yield yourselves to any one as obedient slaves, you are slaves of the one whom you obey . . .? (Romans 6:16).

We should remember two things about a slave. First, he was owned totally by his master. Second, he could therefore have only one master. Both of these observations are difficult for us to comprehend.

We think of working for a person or an institution for possibly eight hours a day. But sixteen hours belong to us. Not so with a slave. All of his time and being was owned by the master. He was never his own. He was so recognized in public, inasmuch as he carried the marks of a slave. There was no way to forget.

In our society, many carry a full-time job and do some "moonlighting" in a part-time capacity. But a slave could have no such divided loyalties. He belonged only to one master.

Paul calls the Christian life a change of masters. We all serve some master. It may be self and sin. Indeed, this is the way we are. To become a Christian is a radical change. We take on a new master in Christ.

What is your ultimate purpose in living? Who finally determines the direction of your existence? Someone does. That one—be he self, Christ, or even another person—is your master.

Serving in Freedom

Although Christ is our master and we are his slaves, Paul makes it clear that we remain free. God does not run a time clock on us. He does not immediately and always punish us when we fail to serve properly.

> But thanks be to God, that you who were once slaves of sin have become obedient from the heart to the standard of teaching to which you were committed (Romans 6:17).

Here Paul teaches that we are obedient to a "standard of teaching," but the analogy is even better in verse 22 where we have become "slaves of God." Our commitment is personal, but it is reflected in our living by a standard. Systematic and disciplined Christian living reflects deep personal and spiritual commitment.

The Benedictine monks enter a monastery in commitment, but they are free to leave at any time during the first year of such commitment. Their clothes with which they came to the monastery are left in their cells, and a monk may change to his previous clothing and leave at any time. He has his clothing removed from the cell and thereby reflects his commitment to a life as a monk, but only after this year in which he can make his ultimate determination.

Many new Christians in our fields of missionary activity undergo an extensive and disciplined period of training before becoming full members of the church. This is particularly true in Zaire (formerly Congo) where a person is committed to a very disciplined Christian life before he can be accepted into the full fellowship of the church.

We follow this practice in some measure in our American churches. Rarely do we accept a person into the membership of the church without his having been involved in a "pastor's class." If one is to make a significant commitment to Christ and his church, it is quite appropriate that he should understand the "standard of teaching" to which he is committing himself as Christ's servant.

Serving with Purpose

In this section of Scripture Paul is generally using the indicative mood. He is describing our situation and the work of Christ for us. On occasion, however, he switches to the imperative, thus exhorting or even commanding us. On the one hand, he tells us what we are by virtue of what Christ has done. On the other hand, he exhorts us to *become* what we already are through Christ's action in our behalf. This is Christ's doing, not ours. Nevertheless, Christ will not do for us that which we have to do for ourselves. We must respond to his action by making it real and functional within our individual and personal experience.

. . . so now yield your members to righteousness for sanctification (Romans 6:19).

41

We are Christ's slaves, but we are free. Therefore we must "yield" ourselves. This is a repeated yielding in daily experience. We need the discipline and practice of living as Christ's people, even though we have already entered into this relationship. This is true of many areas of life. One may learn to play a musical instrument, but he needs to "keep it up." You may learn to speak a foreign language, but you will lose it if you do not use it. We may become competent in a technical sport like golf, but it is only as we maintain our skill through practice that we find great enjoyment in this kind of game. So must we "yield . . . to righteousness."

At the End of the Way

Paul closes this passage by speaking of our ultimate goal which can either be "death" or "eternal life" (Romans 6:23). Our commitment to and relationship with Christ here and now ultimately determines this destiny. Death is the ultimate destruction which comes from our slavery to sin. Eternal life is the ultimate existence into which we move by virtue of our relationship with the eternal Son of God.

For the wages of sin is death, but the free gift of God is eternal life in Christ Jesus our Lord (Romans 6:23).

The words "wages" and "free gift" are terms which were used by the paymaster for the soldiers of Rome. A soldier's "wages" were the pay to which he was entitled by virtue of service and contract. But on certain occasions the emperor made a special "free gift" to such soldiers. This was made at some special occasion or upon a particular recognition of the value of the army. Thus grants were in the form of a bonus or prerecognition.

As Christ's slaves we are under orders, just as are soldiers. But slaves receive no pay. On the contrary, we receive much more. This is not "wages," because we deserve nothing short of death because of our sins. This is rather in the form of a "free gift," because God has graciously granted us the eternal life which none of us deserves.

Victory in Suffering

The first eight chapters of Romans constitute the longest single logical presentation of Christian doctrine to be found anywhere in the Scripture. The climax of this extensive treatise comes in Romans, chapter 8.

It is not strange that this chapter is a favorite of so many people. It was quoted more commonly by the Christian writers for the first two centuries of the church than any other similar section. It is reputed to have been the favorite passage of President Harry Truman and President Dwight Eisenhower. It is certainly beloved by many, and it well deserves to be so.

Romans 8 has been called the chapter of "no condemnation and no separation." The chapter begins with Paul's great affirmation that

There is therefore now no condemnation for those who are in Christ Jesus (Romans 8:1).

The chapter finally concludes with his statement that nothing in all the world

. . . will be able to separate us from the love of God in Christ Jesus our Lord (Romans 8:39).

Thus the chapter begins with our standing fearlessly and without guilt in Christ himself. It ends by indicating that we are secure and inseparably situated in this strong position in Christ. These are great affirmations. There is much to be learned and experienced here.

God Is for Us (verses 31-34)

Since "God is for us" (verse 31), we have need for neither fear nor guilt. First, we need fear no one. "If God is for us, who is against us?" The question is rhetorical, of course. It cannot be answered. No one can stand against us when God is on our side! Second, we need not fear the future. After all, "Will he not also give us all things with him?" The obvious answer is "yes." No matter what comes, God will still be giving. The future is secure. Third, there is no need for guilt. "It is God who justifies," so no one can condemn us. God has already acted as the judge, and he has declared us "not guilty."

> He who did not spare his own Son but gave him up for us all, will he not also give us all things with him? (Romans 8:32).

We cannot conceive of a greater sacrifice than for a person to give up his own son voluntarily. It would be easier to die. One of the reasons that Abraham was considered the spiritual father of the Jewish people was his great devotion to God reflected in his willingness to sacrifice his own son upon God's command (Genesis 22:1-14).

God's response to Abraham's manifestation of devotion is expressed in the well-known words that Abraham had "not withheld your son, your only son . . ." (Genesis 22:16). Note the use of these same words referring to God when Paul says that he "did not spare his own Son." Abraham's devotion to God has only been exceeded by God's great act of love for us. Abraham's son was spared. But our Lord was not. Indeed, he voluntarily took our place so that we might be brought into relationship with the Father.

Paul asks two questions in this passage. Both questions relate to the possibility of our being separated from God. Can we be so separated? This first question relates to *sin*. Will our sin separate us from God? The answer is negative. His love has already overlooked—and indeed overcome—our sin. This second question relates to *suffering*. Can this separate us? Paul lists possible answers which relate to suffering—"tribulation, or distress, or persecution, or famine, or nakedness, or peril, or sword"—and this brings us to our next thought.

Christ Is Close (verses 35-37)

Paul presents Christ as both *representing* us and *relating to* us. He represents us in the presence of God. His representation on our behalf relates to our sins, and his relating to us personally is to deliver us from suffering.

One might feel that the righteousness of Jesus could stand as a condemnation against us because of our sins. On the contrary, however, Jesus "is at the right hand of God," so indeed "intercedes for us" rather than condemning us. The one person in all the world who could have been a proper prosecuting attorney has become our defense. He represents us before the judge of all the earth.

At the same time, however, he is close to us in the midst of our suffering. We are involved in "the love of Christ" which supports us.

Note Paul's realism. He recognizes that suffering is part of our human lot. Moreover, it is rooted in Scripture. Thus he quotes from Psalm 44:22 saying,

> For thy sake we are being killed all the day long;
> we are regarded as sheep to be slaughtered (Romans 8:36).

But we are not delivered from suffering. We are rather protected and delivered in the midst of suffering.

> No, in all these things we are more than conquerors through him who loved us (Romans 8:37).

Note that it is "in all these things" that we are victorious. We are not carried into heaven on flowery beds of ease. We are rather promised the presence of Christ and his love in the midst of the problems which confront us.

Victory Is Sure (verses 38-39)

Our future is sure. Paul concludes this great chapter—and indeed this long section of chapters 1 through 8—with his statement of complete assurance that nothing will be able "to separate us from the love of God in Jesus Christ our Lord" (verse 39). In order to make his point clear, he lists in pairs the greatest conceivable enemies of man which we might anticipate as having the power to destroy us. Note first his great claim in these final two verses. Then we shall consider these specific potential enemies.

> For I am sure that neither death, nor life, nor angels, nor principalities, nor things present, nor things to come, nor powers, nor height, nor depth, nor

anything else in all creation, will be able to separate us from the love of God in Christ Jesus our Lord (Romans 8:38-39).

First, "neither death, nor life" can separate us. Our present life is in Christ. When we die, we go to be with Christ. We should recognize that death is part of our human existence, and as we are in Christ it is not to be feared.

Second, neither "angels, nor principalities . . . nor powers" can separate us. The Jewish people of Paul's time thought there were far more angels in the universe than there were men. Moreover, these angels were considered jealous and hostile toward mankind. Even so, Paul says that Christ is over all these angelic powers, and we need not fear any enmity which they hold.

Third, neither "things present, nor things to come" can separate us. Biblically speaking, there is the present age and the coming age. Even when the new world is established, it will be God's world and the fulfillment of his purposes. We shall be more clearly related to our Lord at that time than now. Thus there is nothing to fear.

Fourth, neither "height, nor depth" can separate us. For Paul and the people of the first century, these were more than vertical opposites. These people (like many today) believed in the power of astrology and horoscopes. The "height" represented the occasion when a particular star was at its greatest strength, and "depth" was that period when a star was preparing to rise in its strength over men. But we are not to fear the powers of astrology. Christ's power is also greater than theirs.

Finally, Paul adds that there is not "anything else in all creation" which can separate us. Great as these opposites may be in their power, the apostle indicates that no conceivable enemy can overcome us. Nothing you can even imagine is great enough to separate you from the love of Christ. You have *victory in suffering.*

Unique Yet Together

So what? Strange as it sounds, this is the emphasis in this section of Paul's letter to the Romans. The first eight chapters present the greatness of God's love and action for us in Jesus Christ. Chapters 9 through 11 relate to the problem of how some (including God's own Jewish people) could reject this great salvation. Beginning at chapter 12 we note the *results* of this salvation in our current life. How ought we to live as a result of our being made right with God?

Pressure to Conform or Power to Transform

All people of Paul's day, Jewish and pagan, offered their sacrifices. An animal was killed and a prescribed ritual was followed in order to meet the desires and demands of the god to whom the sacrifice was made. The Old Testament book of Leviticus describes in great detail the sacrificial system followed by the Jewish people.

I appeal to you . . . to present your bodies as a living sacrifice. . . . (Romans 12:1).

This is different. First, God is not asking for a slain sacrifice. No death is necessary. On the contrary, this is a "living" sacrifice. Second, we are to present ourselves, our own bodies, instead of that of a sacrificed animal. Our lives are called for. The Old Testament demand for a sacrifice of blood was because life is in the blood. Thus it is appropriate that our giving of ourselves be in life as well as in death.

The Greeks of Paul's day would have thought it strange that our "bodies" would be offered to God. They thought of the body as an evil thing. Spiritual freedom was to be achieved when the soul would be set free from the body at death. But Paul emphasizes that we are to serve God in our present life, in the body. This body has been made by God, and it is not evil. Our Lord took upon himself a

47

human body. Just as he served the Father within the realm of the physical, so should we.

. . . your spiritual worship (Romans 12:1).

Our King James Version of 1611 translated these words "your reasonable service." It is not strange that the word "spiritual" could be translated "reasonable" some 350 years ago. Our spiritual activity relates to that non-physical portion of our being. Hence it has to do with the mind or reason.

It seems more strange that the word "worship" could be translated "service." Let us remember, however, that we refer to the church service or to the hour of worship, meaning the same thing. It is more important to see what Paul meant by this word. Originally, the word here translated as "worship" or "service" related to work for which a person was paid. It was what we would call "making our living." Paul is saying that proper worship which is "holy and acceptable to God" is the doing of God's will in daily life. True worship is not limited to incense and altars, organ music and hushed cathedrals. God wants us in the home, in the office, in the shop, and in the classroom. Wherever we go, he is there. Wherever he is, there we serve—and appropriately worship.

Do not be conformed to this world but be transformed by the renewal of your mind. . . . (Romans 12:2).

A more picturesque (and perhaps more helpful) translation of this statement is by J. B. Phillips: "Don't let the world around you squeeze you into its own mold, but let God remold your minds from within." Conformity is the order of the day. Social pressure is all about us. It is difficult not to conform to the customs and behavior of those around us.

But the dedicated Christian is different. We are to determine our existence from within. The concerns of God transform our thinking and our doing. To be a Christian is to be right with God. To live the Christian life is to reflect this rightness in a world to which such activity may seem foreign.

48

Unity in Our Differences

We are one in Christ. Nevertheless, we are different. These two emphases are made clear in the twelfth chapters of Romans and First Corinthians, as well as in other sections of the Bible. It may sound contradictory to say that we "though many, are one," but these are the exact words which Paul uses both in Romans 12:5 and 1 Corinthians 12:12.

This is hardly a contradiction. Consider the analogy of your own body. It is composed of many members. They are of different size, sensitivity, and function. But they are a unity in a single body.

This was also true of the political situation of Paul's day. There were many different countries and provinces. There were numerous kings and local rulers within that world. But there was one Roman government to which all were subject. There was great diversity in the Roman world, but there was also great unity.

This is also true of countries such as the United States and Canada. Some United States' coins still bear the motto *e pluribus unum*—"out of many, one." These countries contain many states or provinces and their citizens come from many different backgrounds. But the United States of America is one country and Canada is one country.

So the church. We are all different people, but we are the body of Christ. This is one body, and we are members one of another.

Our differences are in both background and function. Our differing backgrounds are emphasized in 1 Corinthians 12:13. We are "Jews or Greeks, slaves or free." But we are "one body." In Romans 12:4 Paul speaks of our different *functions*. Clearly "all the members do not have the same function," but we are "one body."

Paul's emphasis is upon our *unity* even while he observes our differences of background and function. The great Greek philosopher Plato also dealt with the theme of unity and diversity within the human body. He pointed out that you would not say, "My back has a pain." Instead you would say, "I have a pain in my back." Even

49

though your back is only one part of your body, it is still part of you. When any single member of your body hurts, you hurt.

Using Our Abilities

Our abilities and talents are gifts from God. But these gifts are not ends in themselves. They are means for something greater. These gifts are given to us as individuals, and they are as different as we are as individual persons. But these gifts are to be used for the benefit of the one body, the fellowship of Christians of which we are a part.

Having gifts that differ . . . let us use them . . . (Romans 12:6).

We are not to be satisfied in knowing that we have received gifts. Neither are we to be pleased by noting the distinctiveness of our individual gifts. Rather we are to use them.

Note the listing of the gifts which Paul suggests in Romans 12:6-8. He lists seven specific gifts: (1) prophecy, (2) service, or ministry, (3) teaching, (4) exhortation, (5) contributing, (6) giving aid, and (7) acts of mercy. But we have taken all of these gifts (except that of "contributing"), and we have related them to the work of the pastors of our churches. We act as if ministers are to do the preaching, teaching, ministering, and showing mercy by visitation to those in need. Indeed, the ministers have also accepted these responsibilities as being uniquely theirs. And we are all wrong. Paul says that these are gifts of all of us. Whatever your gift, use it!

We must recognize that we are now Christ's body. He is no longer in the flesh. If he wants to preach, to teach, or to help people in need, he must do it through you and me. Christ has no hands in this world other than yours or mine. He has no other voice through which to speak. It is not strange that when Paul speaks of gifts he quickly adds that we must "use them."

Living Victoriously in Society

We all have problems. We all experience conflict. We should expect it to be so for at least two reasons. First, we are human. That means we are different from one another. Second, we are sinners. Our self-centeredness inevitably increases our problems and enhances the conflict to which we are naturally drawn.

Share: In Joy or Sorrow

In Romans 12:14—13:1 Paul calls to our attention some important areas of conflict in life. He further indicates how we should respond to these conflicts.

First, he refers to a way we relate to our Christian brothers and sisters.

Rejoice with those who rejoice, weep with those who weep (Romans 12:15).

We would normally think that the area of rejoicing is not a problem, whereas the area of sorrow and weeping is. Not so. It is usually easier to identify with a person in sorrow than it is to identify with a person experiencing great joy and success.

It is not easy honestly to "rejoice with those who rejoice." There is, for example, the inevitable envy which we experience in observing the success of another. Note the difficulty of congratulating the man who achieved the position which you had hoped you might be asked to fill. How do you slap a person on the back and rejoice with him at the point of his raise in salary when inside you feel that you were more deserving? It is not easy to offer best wishes to the girl who has just become engaged when you wonder if *you* will ever hear that desired proposal. Even while you share the joy of a woman who has just brought forth her first child, you may well sense an envy within if you have never held your own baby in your arms.

It is especially difficult to rejoice in a success which is at your expense or is one which you desired for yourself. But

Paul is clear. We are to rejoice and share with our brother or sister. His exhortation is without compromise.

It is easier to feel honest sympathy for a person in the midst of sorrow. The difficulty is how to express this sympathy. We may feel that we should avoid the person who is in sorrow, but this reflects our own anxiety about the situation. Paul does not ask that we have great verbal skills and an ability to explain the problem in which a person is involved. He rather asks for an identifying action. We are simply to "weep." But if the tears don't come naturally, we can simply be there! Just your presence, the touch of your hand, may be the needed thing at that time of crisis.

Avoid Conceit

We are not only to relate to those with whom it is easy; we are also to relate to those less desirable people—the ones with whom it is more difficult to identify.

> Live in harmony with one another; do not be haughty, but associate with the lowly; never be conceited (Romans 12:16).

As Christians, we should recognize that there really is no one that is undesirable. Every person is created in God's image. Every man, woman, and child is so important that Christ gave his life for that one. Hence we have no reason to "be haughty."

Paul does not recognize any person as undesirable. He rather exhorts us to "associate with the lowly." He is not referring to inferior people, but rather to those who are in a lower social or economic level. We should associate with such people without patronizing. The fact is that we can learn much from those who are "not our kind." Moreover, every person *is* our kind. The church of Jesus Christ is composed of people . . . "from every tribe and tongue and people and nation" (Revelation 5:9). Our haughtiness or conceit reflects not our superiority, but our inner feelings of inferiority. The reason we "put on airs" is that we feel inadequate. We must impress people. Our conceit is really a "cover up." It is usually the smallest dog that yelps the loudest!

Avoid Vengeance

Paul also indicates how we are to relate to a persecuting individual or group. His teaching, like that of our Lord, is one of "turning the other cheek." Because this reaction to persecution is the most difficult to accept and live by, he deals more extensively with this particular concern (Romans 12:14, 17-21).

Paul clearly teaches that we are to relate positively toward those who would be our enemies. We should "bless and . . . not curse them" (Romans 12:14). We are to "never avenge" ourselves (Romans 12:19).

Paul gives us three reasons for avoiding vengeance. First, it is not our business. Taking vengeance is usurping the right of God.

"Vengeance is mine, I will repay, says the Lord" (verse 19).

Second, vengeance will not change your enemy. It only enhances the vicious circle of hatred. Only forgiveness has a chance of changing the "enemy" and stopping the feud. Third, to take vengeance is to be caught up in evil. Do not be overcome by evil, but overcome evil with good" (verse 21).

No, "if your enemy is hungry, feed him; if he is thirsty, give him drink; for by so doing you will heap burning coals upon his head" (Romans 12:20).

This statement does not mean that we are to punish a person. Quite the contrary. Paul's point is that we should not take vengeance. This statement probably refers to the Egyptian practice of carrying a pan of burning charcoals on one's head publicly as a sign of penitence. In any case Paul is clearly teaching that we should not react to evil vengefully and thus increase the hatred of an evil person. We are rather to work for his repentance and therefore "overcome evil with good" (verse 21).

If possible, so far as it depends upon you, live peaceably with all (Romans 12:18).

Paul recognizes that this life of peace with every person is not easy. It is hard to be like our Lord. Paul is realistic. Hence he admits to two possible qualifications. First, we are so to live "if possible." Second, we are to live in peace "so far as it depends upon you." It not only takes two people to fight; it takes two to make peace. This softens the demand of Paul, but we must be careful not to soften this Christian grace beyond these realistic qualifications of Scripture. We are far more likely to err in the other direction.

Avoid Anarchy

Paul also indicates how we are to relate to governing authorities. We should be good citizens.

Let every person be subject to the governing authorities (Romans 13:1).

We should note two things. First, Paul is referring even to poor governments. He was writing this at the time when Nero (a notoriously evil ruler) was the world dictator. Second, Paul stated that governments "that exist have been instituted by God." He is referring to their existence rather than their nature. God wills that there be governments, but he does not will that there should be bad governments. Scripture clearly teaches that we should not be anarchists, but we should improve the situation in which we find ourselves.

Paul could have taken other positions. He could have agreed with the Jewish Zealots, who were revolutionaries. They did all that they could to overcome the government of Rome. On the other hand, he could have identified with the Jewish Essenes. They withdrew from society and lived their own lives apart from all human government. He could even have taught that love is the basis of life and we need no law and government. But Paul rightly said that government as such is given by God. Thus we are to live and work toward making ours the best possible state under God.

With Malice Toward None

In Romans 14 Paul expands his teaching concerning Christian love which was begun in chapter 12 and to which we have already given attention. He now turns to love in practice as it relates specifically to our Christian brothers with whom we disagree. In 1 Corinthians 8 he also deals with the matter of disagreement among Christians—in this case as to whether Christians should or should not eat meat which had been offered in a pagan temple.

Accept Differences (Romans 14:1-2; 1 Corinthians 8:7-8; Galatians 2)

We cannot—indeed we should not—expect that all Christians will think and act in exactly the same way. If we limit our thinking, for example, simply to the matter of diet, we find at least three areas of disagreement among Christians in Paul's letters.

First, in Romans 14 Paul discusses the disagreement between meat eaters and vegetarians. There were some Christians who refused to eat any meat (as a committed Seventh Day Adventist refuses today).

Second, in 1 Corinthians 8 he discusses the disagreement between those who would eat only meat which had not been sacrificed in a pagan temple and those who would eat meat so sacrificed. Both groups would eat meat. The only question was whether or not the meat had been offered in pagan worship.

Third, in Galatians 2 Paul describes the disagreement between Jewish Christians who would eat only kosher meals and those who felt freed from such dietary restrictions. This difference continues to exist even today among members of the Jewish community. The more strict and Orthodox Jews will only eat foods which are prescribed by Scripture and tradition. Such foods must be prepared according to the standards communicated by rabbis. This third situation is not our primary concern in today's church.

Paul makes his own position clear in the two disagreements reflected in Romans 14 and 1 Corinthians 8. He agrees with those who eat meat, Romans 14. He also agrees with those who are willing to eat meat which had been offered before an idol, 1 Corinthians 8. In neither case, however, does he "put down" the people who disagree. They have a right to hold the position which seems best to them.

It is important that we recognize that there are areas in life in which there is neither a right nor wrong position. Things are not always black or white or crystal clear. There are varying shades of gray, and we should not be dogmatic in such areas. Take a few moments to enumerate any practices which are in this category as they relate to your particular church and circle of acquaintances. It is important to apply the emphases of this section to these modern concerns. The specific situations have changed, but the basic principles remain the same.

Be Tolerant (Romans 14:3-4)

> Let not him who eats despise him who abstains, and let not him who abstains pass judgment on him who eats; for God has welcomed him (Romans 14:3).

Paul's admonition to both groups in this disagreement is to be tolerant. The other person is far more important than our particular position in this matter. In this particular disagreement the more liberal persons are in danger of despising those with whom they disagree and calling them "narrow-minded." On the other hand, the other group would think of the more liberal persons as being uncommitted, morally loose, and deserving of censure. Sound familiar?

Paul goes to the heart of the matter:

> . . . welcome him . . . for God has welcomed him (Romans 14:1, 3).

He then goes on to indicate that this person is God's servant. We have no business criticizing the servant of another. Our criticism of a brother or sister in Christ is an attack upon his Master. Who are you to pass judgment on the servant of another?

> It is before his own master that he stands or falls. And . . . the Master is able to make him stand (Romans 14:4).

We must remain open to the loving purpose of God.

Christians can differ while not being wrong even today. We have no right to reject a person because of the length of his hair, the style of his dress, his political affiliation, his ethnic background, his language, his color, or the life style in which he expresses his Christian commitment and freedom. We may be shocked to find German Christians who drink beer or Dutch Christians who smoke cigars. But we should remember that other Christians are scandalized by the fact that we have organ music in our worship services or even that we drive automobiles! These differences may be real, but they do not relate to the gospel. People may differ from us, but they are not necessarily wrong.

Be Sensitive (1 Corinthians 8:9-13)

Paul has an additional admonition to those of us who may be broader in our outlook in one of these areas of honest Christian disagreement. This admonition is that we be sensitive to the outlook and needs of the other person. We must consider the effect of our words and actions, inasmuch as they may harm our brother's relationship to Christ. We can be wrong in spirit and action even if we are right in our understanding and doctrine.

In Paul's day a Corinthian Christian could be so sensitive to meat which had been offered in a pagan temple that he could "eat food as really offered to an idol" (1 Corinthians 8:7). In other words, he felt that he was actually worshiping the pagan god by eating such meat. Other Christians (including Paul) recognized that there was no such god and that such meat was therefore no different from any other meat.

Note that Paul does not try to argue for one position or the other. He is only concerned about our continuing growth in Christ and as Christian brothers. The sensitive brother will be helped only if the stronger brother is willing to understand and appreciate the sensitivity.

Therefore, if food is a cause of my brother's falling, I will never eat meat, lest I cause my brother to fall (1 Corinthians 8:13).

Paul refuses to flaunt his freedom and knowledge at the expense of his weaker brother.

If we use our knowledge and ability at the expense of another Christian, we shall find ourselves far from Paul's (not to say our Lord's) attitude toward people.

And so by your knowledge this weak man is destroyed, the brother for whom Christ died (1 Corinthians 8:11).

We are not to think only of ourselves, but of our brother. It has been well said that my rights end where my brother's nose begins! He too is God's concern, and he should be mine.

We should be careful, however, not to become enslaved to another person's silly scruples. If we carry Paul's principle too far, we shall avoid stepping on cracks in the sidewalk, because another person is superstitious. We shall be forever driving around the block, because a black cat crossed our path and another person is disturbed.

We could therefore become involved with all kinds of pagan superstitions simply because our weaker brother refuses to allow us our proper freedom in Christ. Remember that Paul is talking about the possibility of *idolatry* here. He is not simply dealing with the brother's viewpoints. He is dealing with a brother's understanding of and moving away from a commitment to Christ.

Paul speaks of the broader person who is willing to receive his brother as being *strong*. Indeed, it takes great strength to be tolerant and accepting of the brother with whom we disagree. It takes even greater strength to be sensitive to his needs and support him in his Christian growth even while we disagree with him. But this is the kind of strength which was so clearly shown in our Lord Jesus Christ.

Don't Lose Heart

In 2 Corinthians 4, Paul at once recognizes the greatness of our ministry and the weakness of us who minister. Thus he contends that

. . . we have this treasure in earthen vessels, to show that the transcendent power belongs to God and not to us (2 Corinthians 4:7).

Paul continues the thought in this passage. This distinction between the greatness of the ministry and the weakness of the ministers is not permanent. All of us have a ministry. On the one hand, we are in process of becoming weaker and moving more toward that point we call death. On the other hand, there is a constant and positive growth of our inward nature which is both spiritual and eternal. We grow older and weaker, but we also move toward that day when our spiritual strength will be complete and we shall be like and with our Lord Jesus Christ.

Understanding Our Future Life

We are naturally curious about the future. A sure-fire way to increase church attendance is to announce a sermon on "prophecy."

But God doesn't work this way. The Bible never answers all our questions about the future. Many of the details are missing from the picture. We don't even know the time. But we do know the fact. More important, we know him who is at the center of the fact. We know that he will come again and consummate all of God's purposes at the end of our human history.

In 2 Corinthians 5, Paul describes "a heavenly dwelling" for each of us as we move into eternity. We would at least like to know *when* we move into this "building from God." Will it be at the moment when we die? Paul doesn't answer our question. Will it be at the great resurrection? Again, no answer. Will it be at the second coming of Christ? Still no answer. Our need of affirmation is met. But our curiosity is dismissed. He gives no answers to the unnecessary questions.

Paul rather gives us two pictures concerning the future. On the one hand, "We have a building from God" (verse 1), a "heavenly dwelling" (verse 2). On the other hand, he anticipates that we shall "not be found naked" (verse 3), but that we shall "be further clothed" (verse 4). He therefore pictures our future condition as both an eternal building in which we shall dwell and as a new type of clothing in which we shall live. Note again that this helps our understanding of our future state, but it fails to clarify our curious demands concerning the details. The glory and mystery of our great future remains. We know that we shall see him and be with him, but there will still be that joyful surprise relating to the many unknown items.

> . . . we sigh with anxiety; not that we would be unclothed, but that we would be further clothed, so that what is mortal may be swallowed up by life (2 Corinthians 5:4).

When Paul desired "not that we would be unclothed, but . . . further clothed," he was disagreeing with almost all the Greek and Roman thinkers of his day. They looked toward death as being unclothed. The body was considered a prison house of the soul, and these people wanted to be freed from the body. It was considered something evil. Even the highly moral Stoic philosopher of Paul's day, Epictetus, said, "You are a poor soul burdened with a corpse."

In our own day many are attracted to the Hindu thought of a heavenly nirvana which is the quietness of becoming extinct. But Paul is not desiring any escape from the reality of either a bodily or an individual existence. He is not seeking to become a disembodied spirit or to be fading into the nothingness of the divine. He rather anticipates that time when God will give him a new existence in the form of a body equipped for the spiritual dimension. Then he, and we, will be able to relate to and serve God in a fuller capacity than we have ever known.

Indeed, Paul is anxious about the possibility that he "would be unclothed." He rather looks with excitement to "be further clothed." He is using more than the picture of clothing. He is really expecting ". . . that what is mortal may be swallowed up by life" (verse 4). We shall be involved in the very life of God which is eternal in its dimension.

Certainty Concerning the Future

Not only do we understand in broad outline the new kind of life which God has prepared for us. We may be certain of it. Moreover, this certainty is rooted in present experience. We have already entered into this life.

. . . God . . . has given us the Spirit as a guarantee (2 Corinthians 5:5).

Our present experience of the Holy Spirit within is anticipatory of that fuller experience of God's presence which we shall know in the life to come. We have anticipated this in the gospel song "Blessed Assurance." There we sing of "a foretaste of glory divine." Rightly so! Our knowledge of Christ, our experience of God's Spirit, in the here-and-now is in a measure what the full knowledge of God will be at large.

Paul speaks of the Holy Spirit as "a guarantee." Our older translations used the word "earnest." This is something like a down payment. It is an amount given as a promise of fuller payment at a later date. Thus the experience of the Holy Spirit is a promise of future fullness.

This word may be better understood when we recognize that the Greek term is used by modern Greeks to refer to an engagement ring. When a young man gives a girl his promise of love and devotion in the form of this ring, he is giving a portion of his heart and life as a promise of fuller things after the marriage.

Present Strength in Future Hope

Every day we are older. We are nearer death. But there is another side to the picture. Every day we are becoming more mature. As Christians, we should be more Christlike with every new spiritual experience.

So we do not lose heart. Though our outer nature is wasting away, our inner nature is being renewed every day (2 Corinthians 4:16).

If we look at our movement toward death, we might "lose heart." But if with Paul we note our continuing spiritual renewal, then "we do not lose heart." Indeed, the problems and sufferings which may weaken us physically can also develop spiritual strength.

Death for Paul was not something to be feared. The early Christian martyrs went so far as to look forward to death with joy. We may feel that they carried this anticipation too far, but we must share their refusal to look upon death with untoward fear. Death is really part of the life which God has given us. But it is only a part. For the Christian it is a stepping into a fuller kind of life. It is interesting to remember that in all four Gospels Jesus never referred to his coming death without also mentioning the resurrection. His death was given to him by the Father, and it related to an even fuller life. Our death is similarly given, and we should so think of our coming life.

By noting the future with this attitude, we gain strength for even the difficult experiences of the present. There is nothing which shall be able to defeat God's purposes within our life. We live while listening to another drummer. Our citizenship is ultimately in another land.

Our assurance of the future and enjoyment of the present should strengthen the sinews of our service. Not only is our future in his hands; even our present resolve and activity are rooted in and drawn by the love which we already know.